Collins Care for your

RSPCA
PET GUIDE

Budgerigar

Contents

New 3rd Edition
First published in 2005 by
Collins, an imprint of
HarperCollins*Publishers*
77-85 Fulham Palace Road
Hammersmith, London W6 8JB

The Collins website is www.**collins**.co.uk

Collins is a registered trademark of HarperCollins Publishers Limited

10 09 08 07 06
10 9 8 7 6 5 4

First published as *Care for your Budgerigar* in 1980 by
William Collins Sons & Co Ltd, London

Second edition published in 1990

Reprinted by
HarperCollins*Publishers*
and subsequently reprinted 12 times

The RSPCA is a registered charity (no. 219099)
The RSPCA website is www.rspca.org.uk

Designed by: SP Creative Design
Editor: Heather Thomas
Design: Rolando Ugolini

Photographs:
David Alderton: pages 6 and 31
Dennis Avon: pages 3, 12, 15, 18, 22, 23, 32, 42, 45 and 46

A catalogue record for this book is available from the British Library

ISBN-13 978 0 00 719358 5
ISBN-10 0 00 719358 0

Colour reproduction by Colourscan
Printed and bound by Printing Express, Hong Kong

Foreword

Owning budgerigars is great fun but also a huge responsibility. All pets need a regular routine and lots of love and attention. But, most importantly, pets need owners who are going to stay interested in them and committed to them all their lives.

Anyone who has ever enjoyed the company of a pet knows just how strong the bond can be. Children learn the meaning of loyalty, unselfishness and friendship by growing up with animals. Elderly or lonely people often depend on a pet for company, and it has been proved that animals can help in the prevention of and recovery from both physical or mental illness.

The decision to bring a pet into your home should always be discussed and agreed upon by everyone in the family. Bear in mind that parents are ultimately responsible for the health and well-being of the animal for the whole of its lifetime. If you are not prepared for the inevitable expense, time, patience and occasional frustration involved, then the RSPCA would much rather that you didn't have a pet.

Being responsible for a pet will completely change your life but if you make the decision to go ahead, think about offering a home to one of the thousands of animals in RSPCA animal centres throughout England and Wales. There are no animals more deserving of loving owners.

As for the care of your pet, this book should provide you with all the information you need to keep it happy and healthy for many years to come. Enjoy the experience!

Steve Cheetham MA, VetMB, MRCVS
Chief Veterinary Officer, RSPCA

Introduction

The budgerigar is actually a small species of parrot, which is native to Australia, where it roves over the semi-arid interior plains in vast flocks. During the nineteenth century, naturalists introduced the budgerigar into Europe, where its popularity grew to such an extent that it was soon in great demand as an exotic pet.

Throughout the nineteenth century, nets were laid out on their feeding grounds to catch the wild budgerigars as they came down to feed on seeding grasses. Those that survived the traumatic experience of being netted were transported to Europe, where they were bred and became the ancestors of today's domestic budgerigar. All budgerigars now offered for sale have been bred in captivity.

Budgerigars do not build nests. In the wild, they lay their eggs in any convenient place, such as a hollow tree, which affords protection and enables them to roll the eggs during the incubation period. Given suitable nesting boxes inside a breeding cage, budgerigars can be bred successfully in captivity.

Budgerigars as pets

Caged budgerigars are less fortunate, but they do make particularly good pets for a family with very limited space and possibly modest means. If possible, you shoud keep a pair of budgerigars in a good-sized cage. It is essential that caged birds should be given some daily exercise out of the cage. When a budgerigar has to be kept on its own, it will need the stimulation of appropriate toys and also plenty of human contact. Young budgerigars may learn to talk if they receive lots of encouragement before the age of six months.

Endearing companions

Budgerigars are cheerful, hardy companions, which respond well to training and human companionship and develop distinctive characters. Just how much individuality they show will depend, as with all pet animals, on the degree of freedom that they are allowed, and on the stimulation that is provided by their surroundings and their companions. The only time when fit budgerigars lack vitality is when they are moulting, which seems to be very debilitating for a short while.

There are now thought to be six million of these agreeable little birds in Britain alone – but, as with all other birds that are kept in captivity, they need to be provided with the appropriate care.

Budgerigars in the outback

The vast, semi-arid grasslands of the Australian interior are the natural home of the budgerigar. It is a migratory bird, spending summer in the cooler south of the continent and then flying north for the winter. Within this general annual pattern, however, flocks of birds are constantly on the move, partly to find fresh sources of food and water and partly to avoid the excessive heat. Unlike many other migratory birds, such as swallows, budgerigars do not return to the same site every year. They are opportunistic rovers.

The typical vegetation of the budgerigar's favoured environment is scrub grass, which provides food when it seeds, and eucalyptus trees, which provide valuable shelter and nesting places. Budgerigars' water requirement is relatively low, but a supply is, of course, essential. Their need to conserve water is reflected in the fact that they excrete very little, resulting in almost dry droppings.

The natural breeding season is from October to December. During the incubation period, the cock feeds the hen, and he helps with the feeding of the young by dehusking seeds for them. The learning phase of the young chick's life is extremely intense, and at six weeks it is fully fledged and ready to migrate with its parents.

▶ The wild budgerigar's bright green plumage and the contrasting wing patterning provide these parakeets with excellent camouflage when they are perching in trees.

Varieties

There are over 100 different colour varieties that are recognized by budgerigar breeders, all produced by selective breeding from mutants of the wild light green type. For owners who do not wish to breed from their birds, the choice of a particular colour is a matter of personal taste. The longevity or good health of the colour varieties does not differ significantly.

Light green

Wild budgerigars are generally light green in colour, with a yellow mask, shoulders and wings. The six throat spots, the wing and head markings are black. The domestic Light Green variety is closest to the wild type, but it is larger. Different colours, such as light yellow or dark green, will appear naturally from time to time in a wild flock, but the new sports, or mutations, tend to die out in the wild.

Basic colour series

In captivity, the mutant forms, when they occur, are 'fixed' by breeding the mutant back to its offspring. The four colour series are Blue and White, which have a white ground colour, and Green and Yellow, which have a yellow ground colour.

There are three shades of each colour. The three shades of the Blue series are Sky Blue (light), Cobalt (medium) and Mauve (dark). The three Whites are White Sky Blue (light), White Cobalt (medium) and White Mauve (dark). In the Green series, the succession is, confusingly, Light Green (light), Dark Green (medium) and Olive Green (dark). The yellow follows this same classification.

◀ Cobalt cock (left).

◀ A Light Sky Blue and Light Green cock (far left).

▶ This Albino cock is actually a mutation which results from a lack of pigmentation.

▶ Green and Yellow cock (opposite)

Colour factors

The basic colour series are modified by the Grey, Slate and Violet colour factors, which occur in the light, medium and dark shades. There are, for example, Grey Greens, Grey Dark Greens and Grey Olive Greens. The Slate factor also modifies the basic colours slightly. The Violet factor does not make a bird that colour, except in the Violet Cobalts, but it intensifies the colour.

Albinos and Lutinos

Albinos and Lutinos are mutations resulting from a lack of pigmentation. Blues and Whites, which have a white ground colour, produce Albinos. Mutation of the yellow ground colour of Greens and Yellows produces an entirely yellow bird, the Lutino. Both types have red eyes.

Pied budgerigars

Pied varieties, which are sometimes called Variegated or Harlequin budgerigars, have broad bands or patches of a second colour over parts of the body. Frequently, the upper chest is yellow, with a band of green below. In the Blue series, the chest is banded blue and white. Grey and yellow-faced characteristics are also not uncommon.

Opaline budgerigars

Budgerigars that have the standard pattern of markings are known as 'normal'. Opalines, however, are a mutation and show variations of the standard pattern. Ideally, there are no head markings and the body colour and the ground colour of the wings correspond. The Opalines' most distinctive feature is a large V-shaped area of pure colour with no markings, which is called the mantle, between the wings.

Crested budgerigars

There are three types of crested budgerigars: those with a striking flat, full circular crest – like a Norwich canary – which resembles a crown on the bird's head; those with a half crest or fringe, which extends just over the front of the head; and those with a tufted crest in which the feathers are elongated vertically. Crested varieties are uncommon.

▶ Opaline Dark Green hen (right)

▶ Opaline Grey Green cock (far right)

◄ Grey cock with flat
circular crest

Cinnamons and Greywings

Cinnamons and Greywings are bred from mutants which have paler
wing markings than the normal black ones. Cinnamons have a less
intense body colour than normal, and the head and wing markings
and throat spots are reduced to a light cinnamon brown. In Greywings,
all the black markings are reduced to an attractive shade of light grey
and the body colour is also paler than normal

Other varieties

Budgerigars come in an amazing range of colours and varieties,
including Fallows, Lacewings, Spangles, Clearwings, Whitewings
and Yellow-wings. There are also new mutations, notably the Slate
and the Texas Clearbody.

Biology

Feathers These provide a water-repellent insulation around the body, allowing the budgerigar to maintain a constant temperature. Different feathers, such as the flights and down, are adapted for specialized use. All are attached to muscle for movement. When the feathers are fluffed out, a greater volume of air is trapped close to the body for extra warmth. When they lie flat, this volume of air is reduced. Budgerigars renew their feathers periodically by moulting. Frequent preening keeps them in good condition and completely restores the structure of those that are damaged, for example when the interlocking barbules are torn apart.

Vent The vent, or cloaca, is a single opening which is common to the reproductive, digestive and excretory systems. The droppings are a combination of faeces and uric acid crystals, which quickly dry out. In general, birds excrete very little water. Budgerigars, in particular, having evolved in the semi-arid conditions of the Australian outback, do not waste water through excretion.

Toes Instead of the typical three toes forward and one backward, the budgerigar's toes are paired. One pair is directed forward; the other backward. This is an aid to climbing and is seen in other climbing birds, notably woodpeckers. The paired arrangement is known as 'zygodactyl', derived from the Greek *zygon*, meaning a yoke.

Wings These correspond to the forelimbs of other land vertebrates. The large surface area needed for successful adaptation to flight is provided by the feathers. These, combined with an extremely light skeleton, give a big wing area with little increase in weight and minimum loss of body heat.

Eyes Birds such as budgerigars, with their eyes set to the sides of the head, have very good sight compared with our own. Our field of vision extends over an angle of about 200°, but only 2° is in sharp focus. Not only is the budgerigar's field of vision much wider, but all the images received, no matter how obliquely, are in sharp focus. The eyes are protected by three eyelids: the upper, the lower, and the nictitating membrane, which is vestigial in man. The budgerigar, however, can close the third eyelid across the front surface of the eyeball for cleaning and for protection.

Beak This is another adaptation to flight. Heavy jaws and teeth are replaced by a beak of lightweight keratin. The variation in form is needed to suit different modes of life and feeding. This shape of beak is common to the parrot family, and is well adapted for removing the husks from seeds. It is also a considerable aid to climbing, and active budgerigars can often be seen using it as such. Sometimes the beak is malformed at birth. When the upper mandible is overdeveloped, relative to the lower, the beak is 'overshot'. When the lower mandible is overdeveloped, it is 'undershot'. Veterinary advice should be sought.

▲ Severely undershot beak

Cere The cere is the exposed waxy membrane at the base of the beak, which is coloured differently, according to sex – blue for the adult male, and brown for the adult female. The term is derived from the Latin *cera*, meaning wax.

Temperature Birds are warm-blooded, or homoiothermic, with a constant body temperature. In the budgerigar this is between 40°C (104°F) and 42°C (108°F). To retain body heat, the bird fluffs out its feathers; to lose it, it increases its normal breathing rate above the normal 80–100 per minute, so that heat is lost through expired air. There are no sweat glands through which water may evaporate on the skin surface to reduce temperature.

Shape The streamlined body shape is, biologically, a necessary adaptation for flight. Breeders value it for aesthetic reasons and count all the following as faults for exhibition purposes: an arched back, a pronounced neck, a paunch, cross wing tips, a protruding beak, thinness and a flattened head.

Choosing a budgerigar

If you are new to keeping budgerigars, what should you choose? For instance, is a male preferable to a female? And is it better to opt for a young or a more mature bird? Male budgerigars are more easily trained than females and are certainly the better choice unless you want to breed from your birds. Young birds can be trained from about six weeks. Older birds may well have been trained but, if this is not the case, they are unlikely to respond after the age of about six months.

Where to buy

A recognized breeder is always the best source of budgerigars. Many breeders are very happy to sell birds that are unsuitable for breeding or showing but are perfectly healthy and are suitable as pets. Birds should never be bought from such outlets as market stalls. See page 33 for information on how to identify a healthy budgerigar.

Checking sex and age

The cere (see page 13) is the key to determining a budgerigar's sex, but sexing a young bird is not always easy and even the experts can make mistakes. In a young male, you will see that the cere is pink, turning blue later in maturity, whereas the young female's cere is a bluish-white and turns brown with age.

The age of a budgerigar is more easily checked than its sex. Young birds have bars of colour from the cere to the forehead or 'cap'. However, these will begin to disappear at about three months of age, when the cere changes colour.

Companion budgerigars

As they are naturally flock birds in their wild habitat in the Australian outback, pet budgerigars will quickly become bored if they are left too much to their own devices. Plenty of human contact with their owner and family, an array of suitable toys and some daily exercise out of their cage (see page 32) will all help to avoid this problem. However, the best way to keep a budgerigar interested and occupied is to provide it with a companion budgerigar. The two birds should be acquired at the same time and housed together to avoid any jealousy. Two males or two females may be kept together. However, if you do keep two birds together, it will not be possible to train them to talk as they will not bond sufficiently to you, their owner.

Aviaries

A well-built aviary is the most satisfactory and attractive housing for budgerigars. They are able to live gregariously, as in the wild, enjoying freedom of movement and some flight, albeit somewhat restricted. An aviary also offers the best possible chance of observing their behaviour in captivity as well as opening up the possibility of keeping compatible species together. Budgerigars must not be kept with small birds, such as canaries, which they tend to bully, but they are compatible with other small members of the parrot family, such as cockatiels, as well as weavers and zebra finches, which are fascinating to keep.

Basic design
Aviaries vary greatly in their design, but the two essential components are an outdoor flight area and a weatherproof indoor sleeping area. Budgerigars are extremely susceptible to draughts, and special care should always be taken in the positioning and the construction of the sleeping quarters to ensure that they are totally draught-proof, but at the same time well ventilated.

Construction
The most usual construction for aviaries is of timber, with wire mesh or weld mesh screens, and a double door for security. For preference, the aviary should be built on a concrete apron, or some similar hard-standing, which can be sluiced down easily, and is rat-proof. Even so, you will have to remain vigilant since rats may attempt to climb the wire mesh and gain access to the aviary through the eaves.

Favoured aspect
The aviary should be sited so that it catches the sun, preferably in the morning or evening rather than the full heat of the day, but part of the flight area should offer shade and protection from the weather at all times.

Furnishings
The sleeping area needs to be furnished with plenty of perching for the number of birds kept, preferably all of it at a uniformly high level. The budgerigar's preference is always for height, and this will prevent any jostling for more favoured positions. Perches should be in a variety of sizes and diameters so that the birds do not get cramp from continually gripping identical perches.

Nesting boxes

Nesting boxes may be provided for the birds in the spring, either in the enclosed sleeping quarters or hung out in the flight area. Essentially, these are secure, dark boxes with popholes and a floor with a hollow in which the eggs will be laid (see page 40). Budgerigars require no nesting material, but a floor lining of sawdust may be provided and will aid cleaning. You should provide more boxes than there are pairs of budgerigars in order to allow for some choice of site, and also

▲ Where space permits, an aviary will allow a number of birds to be kept in much more congenial living conditions than those offered by a cage, however roomy. It should be secure and should include an outdoor flight area and sleeping quarters, which will protect the budgerigars both from the elements and from predators.

position all the boxes at the same height. It is at breeding times that the birds may become quarrelsome, and an odd cock particularly so. However, an unpaired hen is unlikely to be difficult. If it is allowed to do so, almost certainly one of the cocks would raise two families simultaneously, but he would become exhausted in the process and it is therefore always better to keep an equal number of cocks and hens.

Perching

The flight area will needs lots of perching, with some perches, but not all, under the protection of the main roof overhang. Budgerigars

sometimes enjoy a soaking in the rain. Plenty of perching places – far more than would seem strictly necessary for the number of birds kept – will be essential in order to prevent any jostling for favourite positions. We tend to think of budgerigars as being extremely docile birds, but they are capable of being pugnacious with their own kind on occasion. Their particular liking for height should be borne in mind when positioning perches. There should also be a bird table for food pots (see page 20). Other accessories, including the water pots, mineral licks, cuttlefish 'bone', swings, ladders and bunches of seeding grasses can be suspended from the mesh of the wall screens or roof.

◄ Budgerigars generally live very well together in their aviary surroundings, although such birds are not normally as tame as household pets.

Bird table

Seed and water hoppers, sprays of seeding grasses and millet are best distributed throughout the aviary, and can also be placed on a bird table. Squabbling will break out unless the birds have sufficient room to feed without interference from others.

Hatchway

The budgerigars should enter and leave their sleeping quarters by way of a hatch, which should be closed in the evening, when they are all roosting, and opened again early in the morning.

Sleeping quarters

Inside their sleeping quarters, the budgerigars must have adequate perching in a dark, draught-proof area, ventilated by an adjustable grille. Budgerigars are hardy enough to withstand winter temperatures if their sleeping compartment is sturdily built and frost-proof.

Roofing

The height of the aviary is important. Budgerigars like to be able to fly and to perch at a good height, and there should also be adequate headroom for the keeper to work inside the aviary in comfort. The sleeping compartment must be strongly roofed, together with the outside flight area, to give protection to the birds in bad weather.

Hard standing

The aviary is most conveniently sited on an area of hard standing, which should also be a deterrent to rats. Sometimes rats are attracted to an aviary both by the birds and by the presence of their food, and the best aviaries are constructed as rat-proof as possible. Since rats are capable of climbing the wire mesh screens of the flight area, it should not be possible for them to gain access easily at the level of the roof.

Catching aviary birds

Unless an owner spends a great deal of time with the birds, they are unlikely to allow themselves to be handled. Most aviary owners keep a long-handled net for catching their birds should the need arise.

Double security doors

Double doors are a necessary security device to prevent budgerigars escaping. A safety porch should be incorporated whereby one door must always be shut before the other is opened; there must be no space for birds to fly over the inner door. The porch is usually a mesh-covered area which fits around the door leading directly into the aviary. The porch and aviary doors should open outwards from the porch and be bolted.

Caging

Housing budgerigars in a cage is obviously much less satisfactory than in an aviary. As some recompense for their cramped conditions, the birds will need lots of human contact to which they will respond with singing and talking. It is essential that they are allowed a period of free flight – exercise out of the cage – each day, preferably when they are most active, such as in the early morning.

Construction of cage
Choose as large a cage as possible. It should be suitable for housing two budgerigars, with enough room for them to move around it with ease. Manufactured cages are usually made of metal with wire mesh screening. The bars should lie horizontally, to provide a climbing frame. A budgerigar cage that is constructed of timber with a wire mesh or weld mesh front, like the breeding cage which is shown on page 41, has the advantage of being draught-proof and roomy.

Positioning the cage
The cage should never be sited in direct sunshine or in a draught. Many owners find it best to hang the cage on a portable stand that can be repositioned at any time for the comfort of the budgerigar. Birds can become distressed by a smoky atmosphere, and if there are smokers in the house, or an open fire, it is always wise to cover the cage and then remove it to another room.

Free flight
The cage should be positioned in a room where the birds will have human contact and yet can be allowed out of the cage in safety. Other pets and very young children should, of course, be excluded during free flight periods. Windows should be closed and fireplaces guarded even if there is no fire, and any heaters or fans should be switched off. Some house plants are poisonous to budgerigars and they should be removed or covered. If the birds show any inclination to fly into the windows, these should be screened with light-coloured blinds or some netting. Similarly, the door should be hung with either a bead, bamboo or net curtain to create an effective barrier and prevent birds escaping even when it is left open accidentally.

In many small households, where there is no danger of outside doors being left open, the birds can be left free all day to fly and come and go into their cage as they will.

Furnishing the cage

The cage needs to be furnished with perches which are close to each food and water pot, with a high perch for use at all other times. Bought cages are equipped with dowling perches 1 cm ($^1/_3$ in) in diameter, but these are much less satisfactory than a piece of fruit-tree branch, which makes a far preferable natural perch. Any dowling perches need to be kept rough to help the birds maintain their grip. Sandpaper or sand is usually used to line the base of the cage, and ladders, bells, ropes, swings and mirrors are all suitable toys, provided that the cage is not over-furnished with them. Toys made of natural materials, such as wood, are prefererable, as budgerigars tend to peck at their toys, and there is a danger of plastic toys splintering. It will add interest to your budgerigar's life if the toys are rotated so that each day or so a new object is presented to be explored and enjoyed.

▶ If kept indoors, birds need a cage with plenty of room to exercise their wings, and which is easy to clean, well ventilated and equipped with toys.

Feeding and watering

Seed mixture

In the wild, budgerigars feed on seeding grasses, which is why they must be fed mixed seed in captivity. A variety of packeted seed mixes is available. Most are predominantly mixtures of canary seed and millet. The better mixtures are improved by the addition of red rape, linseed or niger, which are particularly nutritious seeds, with a high fat and protein content. Some packeted mixtures have artificial grains added, with additional nutrients.

Budgerigars also welcome some variety in their diet, especially in the form of sunflower seeds and wheat germ, and it is good practice to hang a bunch of seeding grasses for them in their cage.

The budgerigars eat only the kernels of the seeds: the husks are always discarded. For this reason, owners of caged birds should get into the habit of blowing away the husks that the birds deposit on top of their seed containers. It has even been known for budgerigars to starve in a cage where seed was available but it was hidden by a layer of husks.

Fresh green food

In the wild, budgerigars eat fresh green food as well as seeding grasses. From time to time there are very severe thunderstorms in the Australian interior, and although the land is arid, after a

▲ Groundsel

▶ Budgerigars will enjoy millet, which you can buy either as a complete spray or compacted down into a solid cake for them to peck (opposite). They will also appreciate fresh green foods such as dandelion, groundsel or chickweed (right).

▲ Chickweed

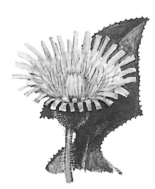

▲ Dandelion

Hygiene

Budgerigars groom themselves, and they do not need any help with this from their owners. However, you must be prepared to set aside some time every day for cleaning out your birds' living quarters.

Daily attention

Each day, your budgerigars will produce quite a litter of droppings, seed husks, uneaten greenstuff and, in the moulting season, feathers, and these should be removed daily. This chore is made much easier if sanded paper is used for covering the cage bottom.

Every day, after the free flight period, you should check the room furniture, surfaces and floors for birds' droppings. These are easily removed using a paper towel, and they will not stain.

Weekly cleaning

At least once a week, the cage will need a more thorough cleaning, and it is convenient to do this while the budgerigar is exercising outside the cage. You should remove all the cage furniture and wash and dry it. Check all the toys for cracks or sharp edges, and remove anything that is damaged. Use a damp cloth or a piece of paper towel to wipe over the cage itself, including all the perches. Check that the perches have not been worn smooth and replace the fruit tree branch if it is necessary. If the perches have become smooth, then it is possible to roughen them slightly with some coarse sandpaper.

Cleaning aviaries

Aviaries demand a more ambitious cleaning programme. Every day, any uneaten food and empty seed husks should be removed, together with any piles of droppings deposited under the perches. The birds' sleeping quarters should also be checked and any droppings, feathers or other rubbish removed from them.

On a weekly basis, the floor of the aviary should be washed down if it is a hard standing one. If not, you should remove the more obvious rubbish and then rake over the surface. All the birds' toys and any other items of furniture should be thoroughly cleaned and checked, and this is a good opportunity to check the general condition of the aviary. You should pay particular attention to weatherproofing, the condition of the wire mesh, and any tell-tale signs of rats.

Cage checklist

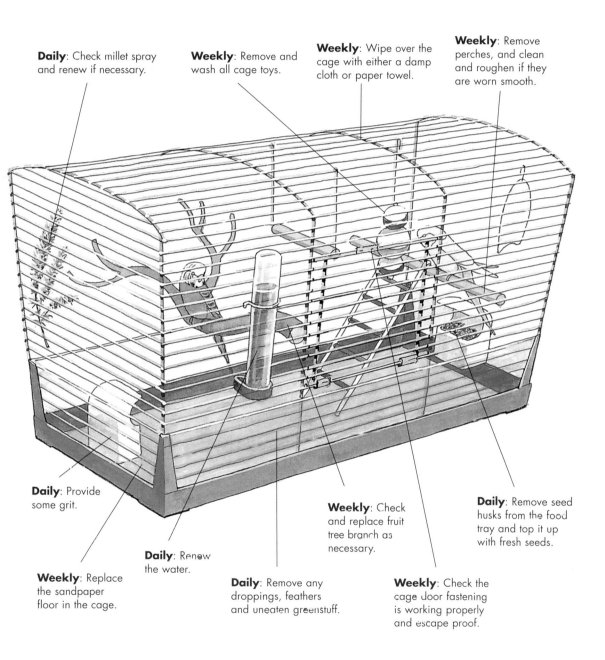

Daily: Check millet spray and renew if necessary.

Weekly: Remove and wash all cage toys.

Weekly: Wipe over the cage with either a damp cloth or paper towel.

Weekly: Remove perches, and clean and roughen if they are worn smooth.

Daily: Provide some grit.

Weekly: Replace the sandpaper floor in the cage.

Daily: Renew the water.

Daily: Remove any droppings, feathers and uneaten greenstuff.

Weekly: Check and replace fruit tree branch as necessary.

Weekly: Check the cage door fastening is working properly and escape proof.

Daily: Remove seed husks from the food tray and top it up with fresh seeds.

Handling and training

The key to the successful handling and training of a budgerigar is to make this the responsibility of just one individual member of the family. Generally, birds will respond best to the pitch of a female's or child's voice, and cocks respond more readily than hens. All handling and training is always best done with no one else present in the room, and no distractions from, for example, the radio or television.

Budgerigars can be handled quite frequently without suffering any stress, but a newly acquired bird should be allowed to settle for a day or so in its new home before being approached by its owner.

Bonding

A single budgerigar will bond to its owner and regard him or her as another member of its flock. This bond can be strengthened by regular attention – conversation, training and handling sessions, and company in general. If the bird has to be left on its own for periods during the day, it can benefit from a radio talk programme at a fairly low volume.

Finger-taming

Finger-taming is the first stage in successful handling, and it should be tried out initially in the cage. You should offer your index finger through the cage door as a perch. All your movements should be slow but deliberate, and your hand must be kept below the level of the bird's head. Many birds will instinctively hop on to the proffered finger, especially if they are encouraged with a few softly spoken words.

An alternative is to hold out a piece of wood as a perch, which some birds will accept more readily. If this is successful, you can try with the finger later. Either way, the exercise should be repeated until the bird automatically accepts the invitation. Once the bird responds confidently within the cage, it may be taken out of the cage. Finger-taming is important as it is a means of returning a bird to its cage after its free flight period. Catching a bird that will not come to the finger may even turn into an exhausting and, for the bird, possibly alarming chase.

Handling and holding

Budgerigars should also be accustomed to being held with one hand gently over their back. The bird's tail should lie along the inside of your wrist, and the head should rest between your first and second fingers. Your thumb and the other fingers can then restrain the wings so that they cannot be fluttered and broken. Once the bird is in position, make a conscious effort to relax your fingers so that your grip is not too tight.

In an emergency, a budgerigar may be caught by dropping a clean cloth over it and then picking it up carefully. If it is necessary to take the bird to the vet, it should if possible travel in its cage. Failing that, you can use a secure box with airholes – suitable cardboard containers can be obtained from pet shops.

Talking

Training a budgerigar to talk must start when it is as young as five or six weeks old. It calls for great patience and persistence on your part, and can be a frustrating business. Some budgerigars will simply never learn to talk, however skilled and patient the trainer.

Training should take place with no other distractions in the room. If the bird is finger-tame, it can be spoken to directly and will give the trainer its full attention. The first word to be taught is the bird's name, which should be chosen for its short, distinctive sound. One word or, later, a short sentence should be taught at a time. The budgerigar learns to imitate exactly what it hears, and for this reason consistency is

▼ A tame budgerigar can be tamed to sit on a finger and will enjoy all the human attention.

essential. The word must always be spoken with the same accent and inflection. The bird will need to hear the word over and over again, and it may not imitate it immediately. In the same way that a young child learns to speak, you may suddenly hear a new word being tried out by your budgerigar long after it was last spoken.

Well-trained budgerigars can build up a considerable repertoire of words and sentences. Particularly good mimics may copy other sounds they hear about the house, such as the ring of the telephone, and may pick up words from people other than their 'official' trainer. Many birds, including some that will not talk, can be taught to whistle tunes.

Playing games

Budgerigars can also be taught to play games with swings, ladders and other toys. The appropriate actions should be demonstrated with your finger, while, at the same time, you give a command such as: 'Have a swing' or 'Ring the bell'.

These handling and training sessions should never be allowed to go on for too long, or the budgerigar will become bored. Ten or fifteen minutes are usually long enough, but you can follow it up with another play session an hour or so later.

▼ Mirrors are popular toys for keeping most budgerigars busy and amused. Some designs are embellished with items, such as sliding beads, as shown here.

The healthy budgerigar

Budgerigars are among the hardiest of birds when they are kept in clean, dry surroundings and fed good-quality food. However, they lose condition fast when they fall ill, so get to know your birds well and you will quickly recognize any change in them. The main signs of health are as follows:

Signs of health

Abdomen	The smooth outline of the bird should be unbroken by hollows, pads of fat, or growths.
Appetite	Feeds mostly early morning: dehusks seed with beak and eats only kernels.
Beak	Should be neither undershot nor overshot; able to dehusk seed. Gasping with beak open is a sign of fever or laboured breathing.
Breathing	This should be quiet and rapid, with the beak closed.
Cere	Waxy in appearance, with no encrustation. After first moult at about 12 weeks, the adult colour shows: blue (male); brown (female).
Claws and feet	Should be no malformation; no encrustation; no overgrown claws.
Demeanour	Bird should be normally quiet and approachable with periods of activity. Alert, observant, imitative and acrobatic.
Droppings	These should be firm; quick to harden.
Eyes	Should be bright and watchful; no discharge; third eyelid not showing.
Feathers	Luxuriant, with none missing (except at times of moult); well-preened and held close to body except when fluffed out in cold spells or in ill health. A good sheen is natural; spiky head feathers a sign of illness.
Forehead	Bar-headed birds, with striations across the forehead, are young birds not yet flighted.
Stance	Bird should sit well clear of the perch, at an angle of 30° from the upright; no hunching or huddling; no loss of balance.
Tail	The long tail feathers are lost twice a year during autumn and spring.
Vent	Should be clean with no staining or scouring.
Wings	Strong, well-feathered, able to support the budgerigar easily in flight.

Siting the cage

Health problems can be made less likely by taking care with the siting of the budgerigars' living quarters. The ideal site in the house for the birds' cage is one where the temperature is most constant. This rules out the kitchen, for example, where there are usually extremes of heat and cold throughout the day and night. Other unsuitable sites include bay windows, which are cold at night and probably draughty, and also passageways. In most households, the best answer is to place the cage in the living-room far away from any windows and doorways, with a light cloth to cover the cage at night.

Exercise

Budgerigars should not be kept as pets unless they are able to exercise daily in free flight. Provided there is no possibility of the birds escaping or coming to harm from dangerous equipment or other pets, they should be allowed as much freedom as possible. If there are children in the house, it is wise to arrange free flight sessions at the same fixed time each day so that doors or windows are not inadvertently opened.

If its cage is large enough, the budgerigars will also obtain some flying exercise there. For this reason, it should not contain too many toys or other obstructions. It is always better to offer the birds a few toys at a time and to change them frequently.

Leaving your pet

As budgerigars need plenty of company, they are unsuitable pets – at any rate as cage-birds – if they have to be left alone for long periods during the day. Also, it is essential to top up and remove the husks from their food supply at frequent intervals. So if you want to keep these endearing birds, you must be around most of the time. If an emergency arises, or when you go away on holiday, you should make adequate arrangements for a friend or neighbour either to look in and feed the birds, or to give them a temporary home. Starvation is a fairly common cause of death in budgerigars.

Going on holiday

If a family is going on holiday in self-catering accommodation, there is no reason why the budgerigars should not be taken along. They can travel in their own cage with a cloth covering, which will encourage them to sleep during the journey. Budgerigars are prone to heat exhaustion which may be brought on by the conditions in a car on a long journey in summer. Make sure that you keep the cage out of direct sunlight and dampen the cover of the cage – a plant spray full of water can be taken to renew the dampness during the journey.

Health problems

It is not difficult to see when a budgerigar is unwell. Typical symptoms include untidy feathers, except during the annual moult, a puffed up or ragged appearance, and a hunched stance. A sick bird may appear sleepy, take little interest in its environment inside or outside the cage, and give up eating. The vent may become soiled from dehusking seed, and the droppings may be streaked with blood. Very often, too, the budgerigar's breathing will be affected (see page 33).

As with most animals, symptoms of ill health set in very quickly, which emphasizes the importance of a daily inspection of birds during their play and training sessions. In general, treatment at home is not advisable. If a budgerigar shows signs of sickness, the best thing to do is to contact your vet, and in the meantime you should make sure that the bird is kept warm, using a cover for the cage if necessary and keeping the bird as quiet and comfortable as possible. If you have more than one bird, isolate the sick one.

Many common health problems can easily be solved by your vet. For example, a budgerigar with an overgrown beak will not be able to pick up enough food and it will rapidly decline. If the beak is clipped by the vet, the bird will begin to eat again and recover within a day or so.

Symptoms of poor health

Hunched back

Head drooping

Cere encrusted

Breathing with beak open

Feathers spiky or untidy (except during moult)

Claws malformed or unable to grip the perch easily

Ailments

It is extremely difficult for an owner to diagnose illness in a budgerigar because the same symptoms, such as a greenish diarrhoea, appear in more than one complaint, including psittacosis. This, and the fact that budgerigars lose condition very quickly when ill, makes it imperative to take prompt veterinary advice.

Scaly face

The grey encrustation that gradually spreads around the beak, cere, eyes, feet and legs is known as scaly face. It is caused by a minute organism which can be killed off by several applications of a germicidal solution or cream, available on veterinary prescription, or in proprietary form at pet accessory stores and counters.

Scaly face is contagious, and an affected bird must always be isolated from all the others.

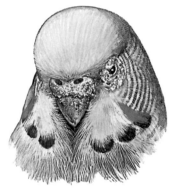

▲ Scaly face with encrustation showing around eyes and cere.

Overgrown beak

Budgerigars, and in particular young budgerigars, will trim their own beaks on a cuttlefish 'bone', which is also a very valuable source of calcium, or by gnawing on fruit tree branches. Sometimes this is not enough to prevent overgrowth, however, and then regular trimming by a veterinary surgeon will be necessary to control the condition which otherwise will eventually prevent a budgerigar from eating at all.

Colds, bronchitis and pneumonia

A budgerigar with a mild respiratory disorder may quickly respond to warmth. If the condition persists, or deteriorates, it will need drugs that are only available on veterinary prescription, and any delay in seeking veterinary help may prove fatal for the affected bird.

The advanced symptoms of colds, bronchitis and pneumonia are very distressing: the bird will sit huddled on its perch, wheezing and gasping for breath with an open beak, and often jerking its tail in a pumping action. Eventually a very sick bird will become too weak even to cling to its own perch.

Red mites

Red mites are a greyish colour during the day; they take on the red colouring after feeding on their host bird during the night. The mites, which affect budgerigars less than they trouble canaries, hide in cracks and crevices during the day and they are almost invisible. Good hygiene is essential here, and only the most rigorous cleaning, including the total immersion of the infected birds' cage, will eradicate a red mite infestation.

Overgrown claws

Sometimes a budgerigar's claws become so overgrown that they need cutting. This is always a job for your vet since for some birds this procedure causes great stress. Nevertheless, it has to be carried out from time to time, although the frequency varies with individual birds.

The necessity for frequent claw clipping can be alleviated to some extent by providing your birds with suitable perches made of fruit tree branches and roughening perches made of machined wood.

Feather plucking

Budgerigars will sometimes peck and preen their own feathers excessively, and this is due to boredom. The habit of feather plucking, once it is established, is difficult to stop. The introduction into a bird's cage of a mirror, play-objects or another budgerigar can often be sufficient distraction to prevent the behaviour.

Tumours

Growths on or under the budgerigar's skin are common, and they have many differing causes. Veterinary advice should be sought in the early stages, since successful treatment is frequently possible.

Regurgitation

This is normal behaviour, and the regurgitation of food by healthy budgerigars should not be mistaken for vomiting. In the absence of a mate, or of young, a budgerigar in breeding condition will regurgitate food over a favourite object in its cage, or over its own feet.

Psittacosis

This is the most serious disease of the parrot family. It is particularly dangerous because it can also be transmitted to humans and may sometimes be fatal if it is not treated early enough. Pet birds, unless they are acquired from infected stock, are unlikely to contract it. If both your bird's eyes are inflamed and it is off colour and showing signs of poor health, you should take it to the vet immediately.

Reproduction

Breeding condition

Mature budgerigars are likely to reach their breeding condition at any time between early spring and early autumn and sometimes during the winter, too. For novice owners, it is important that their budgerigars should only be provided with nesting boxes during the spring and summer, when the young chicks will have the best conditions for development.

A cock bird in breeding condition has a very bright blue cere, and an extremely confident manner. He will pay attention to the hen, and will very likely feed her regurgitated food as if she were already incubating her eggs. A hen bird in breeding condition may also regurgitate food, as if for her chicks, and she will begin to search for a nesting place. It should go without saying that only the best healthy specimens without defects should be allowed to breed.

Clutch size

The normal clutch consists of five or six eggs, with perhaps as many as eight in the first clutch of the year. A good pair of birds may raise as many as three clutches a year, but both the hen and the cock can become exhausted by the demands of excessive breeding and they will produce successively weaker broods. Unfortunately, it is sometimes the young that are produced by excessive breeding that will find their way into the lower end of the pet market. Responsible breeders will control breeding by separating the breeding pair, removing the nesting box or removing the eggs as they are laid.

Egg laying and incubation

The hen will lay her eggs on alternate days and will begin to incubate them from the time that the first one is laid. For this reason, the chicks will hatch at intervals after 18 days' incubation.

The hen will hardly leave the nesting box during the incubation time, relying on the cock to feed her regurgitated seed. When they hatch, the young will be fed in turn by the hen on regurgitated food and a rich 'crop-milk' which has a high protein content.

The young need no hard food provided for them until they leave the nest and begin to feed on normal mixtures. It is vital for the owner to check that the chicks are capable of feeding independently before they are removed from the parents. If they have not made the move to independence, they will starve if they are taken away too soon.

Pairing

Although many budgerigars are biologically ready for breeding at the age of three to four months, they are actually too immature for the strain of rearing before they are ten to eleven months old.

A pair of birds that is normally housed together will usually rear several broods a year, if they are allowed the facilities. In aviaries, the birds will pair up by choice, and great care must always be taken to ensure that there are equal numbers of cocks and hens.

Extra nesting boxes need to be provided for the breeding pairs, or there will be a great deal of squabbling over possession of the most favoured boxes, which are invariably the highest.

▲ A pair of budgerigars with their clutch of six young who will not be ready to leave the nesting box until they are at least four weeks old. They will then need to spend a further two weeks with their parents, until the first difficult task of learning to dehusk seed has been learned.

Nesting boxes and breeding cages

Budgerigars do not build nests in their natural habitat in the Australian outback, nor will they in captivity. In the wild, the birds lay their eggs in the hollows of gnarled eucalyptus shrubs, and they make no attempt to line the holes, even with plucked feathers.

In captivity, however, budgerigars must be provided with a nesting box, such as the one illustrated below, which can be fitted to the side of a breeding cage. In an aviary, there must be a box for each pair of birds, with extra boxes to allow the budgerigars some freedom of choice, and to forestall squabbling.

The depression in the base of the nesting box will hold the eggs, and there is no need to line it or soften it in any way. It is essential that the nesting box has a small round opening for the hen to use, with a perch beneath it. The cock bird will normally use this perch to feed her while the chicks are in the nest.

The front of the nesting box should be fitted with a glass screen behind the wooden door. This enables the interior of the box to be inspected regularly, and the progress of the nestlings noted, without disturbing them or causing them to become chilled.

Droppings accumulate in the nesting box very quickly during the month or more that the young are developing there. If necessary, it is possible to put the nestlings into a cardboard box temporarily, and remove them to a warm place for a short time while the nesting box is being cleaned. This should not be done before the chicks are two weeks old. A dry scraper and kitchen towels should be used to remove the mess, and the nesting box should be kept dry. This procedure also enables the owner to check the condition of the chicks. It may be found that some have droppings caked on their claws or beaks. These may be removed using a kitchen towel dipped in lukewarm water.

◀ A nesting box opened up to show the interior. This is an ideal breeding box for the inside of the cage with a sliding door for easy access, plywood construction without any treatment that could be harmful to birds, a hole for bird access, and a perch and drawer with a concave hole for nesting.

Breeding cage design

Professional budgerigar breeders favour breeding cages of the design illustrated below, which are stackable and relatively easy to construct. The design can be recommended just as well for those budgerigars that are not breeding. Its simplicity, protection from draughts and spaciousness are features that many expensive manufactured cages lack.

Breeding cages may be constructed of timber or hardboard. The wire fronts are constructed of weld mesh. Fronts such as the one in the illustration may be bought separately and fitted to slide into position, or fixed with a separate entrance door for the birds.

Furnishings

The breeding cage does not need furnishing with any mirrors, toys or play objects while a pair of budgerigars is rearing a brood. Boredom is not then a problem, since both the cock and hen have a positive role to play. At other times of the year, birds that are kept in a cage of this design will need it furnished as outlined on page 22.

Nesting box

The nesting box must not be fixed into position until the budgerigars are in breeding condition (see page 38) and the time of year is favourable. Without a nesting box, this cage will provide good accommodation for a pair of birds throughout the year.

Size

The recommended size for the breeding cage is at least 91 x 45 x 45 cm (36 x 18 x 18 in).

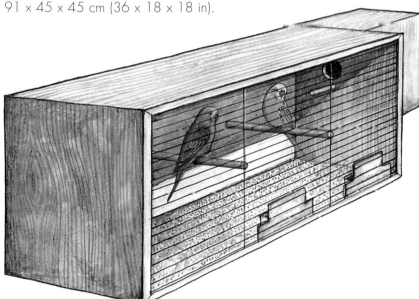

◄ This breeding cage is easy to construct and will be suitable for a pair of birds during the traditional breeding season.

The young

The chicks spend at least the first four weeks of their life in the nesting box, tended by the cock and hen, who are devoted in their care of the young. There are recorded instances of either the cock or the hen dying during the time that their young were still in the nest, and yet the surviving parent still succeeded in rearing the entire brood. It may also happen that if there is a spare hen in a colony of budgerigars, one of the cocks will raise two families, feeding both the hens concerned.

Development of the chicks

When the chicks hatch, they are blind and naked, but by the end of the first week their eyes are open and their feathers are beginning to grow. At four weeks, they are fully feathered, and will soon be sufficiently mature to leave the protection of the nest. At this age they need some help in making the transition to hard food, for they find it difficult at first to dehusk the seed. Again, the cock helps them, until at six weeks they are fully fledged and able to care for themselves. They are ready to be rehomed if necessary. These very young budgerigars have dark horizontal markings across the forehead, which disappear after the first moult at about twelve weeks.

▶ Signs of feathering are now becoming apparent in these eight- and fourteen-day-old chicks. Their eyes have opened.

Sexing and re-homing

Sexing young birds is not as easy as sexing adults. In good health, adult cocks have a blue or violet cere whereas females have a mushroom brown cere. In many juveniles, these colours are not yet distinct and sexing is a matter of guesswork. This accounts for the fact that many people have given a home to a Joey only to find later on she has to be renamed.

Finding homes for budgerigars is not usually as difficult a task as finding homes for many other animals, but it is sensible to allow a breeding pair to raise only a limited number of chicks in a season. Both the cock and hen will become exhausted by the business of raising their young, and they should not be expected to raise more than six to eight chicks in a year. Chicks should never be rehomed singly. Budgerigars are flock birds and a lone budgerigar is never seen in nature.

▲ At six to ten weeks, these budgerigar chicks will be fully fledged and ready to be re-homed. They will moult at about twelve weeks, when the bars across their foreheads will disappear. By this time, males and females should be separated.

Your questions answered

My budgerigar will not take a bath. Have you any advice on how I can encourage him?

Male budgerigars in particular are sometimes reluctant to take baths. However, bathing and subsequent preening are important social and hygienic activities and they should be encouraged. One way is to put a favourite titbit, such as a small piece of lettuce or carrot, in the bird's water so that in order to retrieve it he must get slightly wet and will then preen himself. Alternatively, use a house plant spray on a 'mist' setting, aiming to let the mist fall rather than squirting it directly. It is always important not to overdo it and to allow some time for the feathers to dry before roosting for the night.

As I have been told that a budgerigar kept alone gets very bored, we bought two males as company for each other. All they seem to do is to peck at their own and each other's feathers. What is wrong?

Gentle pecking which does not leave feathers flying is just a sign of companionship. But rougher treatment, perhaps drawing blood, may well be a sign of overcrowding. Here is a check list of points for you. Is the cage large enough? If they peck at each other, they may not have enough personal space. Do the birds have a period of free flight every day? This is essential both for their health and contentment. Do you spend enough time talking to your birds and playing with them? Plenty of human contact is vital. Have you provided an interesting range of toys, which is changed frequently? Is there a variety of perches in the cage?

Can owners catch psittacosis from budgerigars?

Psittacosis is a disease of members of the parrot family with symptoms similar to typhoid. It can be communicated to human beings. It is not endemic in budgerigars but occurs in sporadic and often widespread outbreaks. Cases of psittacosis in humans are occasionally reported, but the risk of catching the disease is generally low. Any unexpected respiratory problems should naturally be checked out by your doctor. At all times, sensible hygiene precautions should be taken.

Will keeping a budgerigar affect my child's asthma?

Always take advice from your doctor before buying a bird. Asthma is unpredictable in its side effects, but health problems are not inevitable. It would be wise to delegate cleaning the cage to someone else to avoid any contact with feather fragments and dust. No budgerigar should be kept in a bedroom, whether the owner is asthmatic or not.

I have recently acquired an aviary, which I am in the process of stocking. Are there any special precautions that I should take in case of a severe winter?

As a general precaution, you should check that the sleeping quarters are draughtproof, especially at the corners and at the wall and roof joints. The aviary should be sited where it gets morning or afternoon sun, if possible with some nearby protection, such as shrubs or a fence, from the worst weather. The birds should, of course, be shut away in their quarters at night. Take care that the aviary is ratproof; it will be particularly tempting to rats if the weather is cold.

My budgerigar always gnaws his sandsheet unless I entice him with a stick of millet. Is there a limit to how much millet he should have?

There is no restriction on millet, but it sounds as if your bird's problem is a lack of grit in the diet. Grit is essential as it is stored in the gizzard and used to digest food. A small container of grit should be available at all times. Check and, if necessary, renew it daily.

I would like to give my elderly mother a pair of budgerigars for her birthday, but I am not sure whether giving pets as presents is a good idea.

Giving pets as presents should always be approached with caution. Sound out your mother first and find out whether she would welcome a couple of budgerigars. Ensure that, if you give her them, they come with all the equipment and initial food, grit and so on that she will need, and that she has a copy of this book. It is not a good idea to introduce pets to a new home at festive times when there may be unusual noise and excitement and routines may be upset. However, having said all this, budgerigars do make excellent, companionable and relatively undemanding pets for elderly people.

Life history

Scientific name	*Melopsittacus undulatus*
Incubation period	18 days
Clutch size	3–10
Birth weight	2 g
Eyes open	6 days
Plumage complete	28 days
Leave nest	28 days (approx.)
Fully fledged	5–6 weeks
Puberty	3–4 months
Adult weight	35–60 g (1–2 oz)
Best age to breed	Males: 10+ months Females: 11+ months
Breeding season	Early spring to autumn
Retire from breeding	Males: 6 years Females: 4 years
Life expectancy	5–10 years